UNPEOPLED EDEN

Also by Rigoberto González

Poetry

Black Blossoms
Other Fugitives and Other Strangers
So Often the Pitcher Goes to Water until It Breaks

Bilingual Children's Books

Antonio's Card
Soledad Sigh-Sighs

Novels

Crossing Vines
The Mariposa Club
Mariposa Gown

Memoir

Butterfly Boy: Memories of a Chicano Mariposa
Autobiography of My Hungers

Short Story Collection

Men without Bliss

Essay Collection

Red-Inked Retablos

As Editor

Xicano Duende: A Select Anthology by Alurista
Camino del Sol: Fifteen Years of Latina and Latino Writing

Unpeopled Eden

Rigoberto González

Four Way Books
Tribeca

Apá
bordercrossing soldier
(1947—2006)

and for the newest soldadito in the family
André
(b. 2009)

Please direct all inquiries to:
Editorial Office
Four Way Books
POB 535, Village Station
New York, NY 10014
www.fourwaybooks.com

Library of Congress Cataloging-in-Publication Data

González, Rigoberto.
[Poems. Selections]
Unpeopled eden / Rigoberto González.
pages ; cm.
ISBN 978-1-935536-36-9 (alk. paper)
I. Title.
PS3557.O4695U57 2013
811'.54--dc23
                    2013004427

This book is manufactured in the United States of America and printed on acid-free paper.

Four Way Books is a not-for-profit literary press. We are grateful for the assistance
we receive from individual donors, public arts agencies, and private foundations.

State of the Arts

NYSCA

This publication is made possible with public funds from
the New York State Council on the Arts, a state agency.

[clmp]

We are a proud member
of the Council of Literary Magazines and Presses.

Distributed by University Press of New England
One Court Street, Lebanon, NH 03766

TABLE OF CONTENTS

En América, you can have the stars también! But you gotta pick them yourself beneath the glare of a scorching moon.

—Anonymous Bordercrosser

THE SOLDIER OF MICTLÁN

Once upon a time there was a soldier
who marched to Mictlán in his soldier
boots and every step was a soldier
step and every breath was a soldier
word. Do you know what this soldier
said? I'd like a piece of bread for my soldier
hand. I'd like a slice of cheese for my soldier
nose. And I'd like a woman for my soldier
heart. The mayor of Mictlán saluted the soldier
and bowed his head as he told the soldier:
We have no bread, oh honorable soldier,
we hold empty hands instead. Dear soldier,
let us take yours if we may. And the soldier
held out his hand to be taken. Oh brave soldier,
said the mayor, cheese is your soldier
wish, but we have none since the other soldier
left. We whiff empty hands instead. The soldier
let the mayor sniff the scent of his soldier
palm. And forgive us, oh strong soldier,
said the mayor, but no woman worthy of soldier
warmth lives in our empty town. Will your soldier
eyes teach us wonder and kindness and soldier
love instead? Silence stiffened the soldier
face as a search ensued in the soldier
head for a moment one moment of soldier
bliss. But all was dead. The longer the soldier
looked the more the streets of his soldier

mind resembled the streets that his soldier
feet had taken him to: where no lost soldier
finds bread or cheese or a woman to be a soldier
wife. This was no space for a soldier
life indeed. So off to the hills the soldier
fled to seek out the place where a soldier
sheds the rattle that beckons the soldier
to death to soldier to death to soldier.

In the Village of Missing Fathers

Children run without shoes
because no bottles have been
broken there and no one knows how
to climb a tree or fly a kite. When the sheets
wave on the line they chirp and sing
and so no reason for feral birds.
No reason for clouds or sky.

When it rains the women never say
it's coming down, they point to the ground
and say it came. No angels hover
because no one wants flight
or things that float without water.
Newspaper boats on the puddle
are the only mystery: they refuse

to sink despite the heavy dream
of travel. They remain mute despite
the casing of words and the memory
of the grief the women poured onto the page
wishing to divine their sons' and husbands'
fates. Each article an obituary, each word
dressed for burial, each page an insult

even to the blue canaries that refuse
to plop their droppings there. And so
in the village of missing fathers
paper sorrow folds into a boat,
a bed into a holding cell for moans
that bleed out of sleep, a house thins out
into a ghost with the smell of Sunday

cologne, with the texture of a scratch
on the arm, with the sound of a throat
ringing after the triumph of carnal
pleasure. And the women watch their children
smear their laughter like paste on
any surface, hoping that something
worth keeping will stick. What wonder,

this collection of objects plucked and kept
in an empty matchbox: a leaf that sprung
out of rock, a bug constricted
in the pellet of a goat, a lock of black hair
tied with red ribbon rescued from the kindling
bucket. And the boys gather around at dusk
to fantasize about its origin: a beauty from

some other village, no doubt, perhaps
a dancer who can point to the ceiling
with her toe while standing on the other
foot, perhaps a princess who wears silver
to bed and who sips tea made from flakes
of gold, perhaps a lady whose gown
cascades with light, whose hands only need

the strength to lift an ivory comb.
But certainly not any woman from here,
the village of missing fathers, where women
have traded their silks for meats, their kisses
for bolts on the doors, the curves
of their hips for a place to carve out
the names of the dead. The boys have caught

glimpses of such scarred tissue, and it
shamed them into never watching anyone else's
mother disrobe again. Not while they soak
their bony bodies in the bath and rise
one shade darker. Not while they slip
from one black cloak into another,
the momentary flash of flesh a sad

accident, like a foot falling on
the only daisy left standing after the cow
stampede. And certainly never at night
while their mothers lie in the hollow
of the mattress and roll their torsos
in the final trace of musk that must have
overwhelmed them once, when they were

wives. Oh delicious weight of passion,
oh terrible tickle, oh precious probe.
The women are becoming brittle without it.
The boys are growing anxious with it.
The walls of every house are threatening
to collapse from the negligence of it.
But no, beloved ones, never worry,

the sad architecture of abandonment
will always stand. The broken world
spins this way: a woman runs afraid
out to the street at midnight and the moon
stops her by stepping on her braid
and all the other women come to clothe her
with shadow. The town priestess prays for her

until the woman understands that muscle
crushed to bone will take the place of touch.
And the woman hardens her resolve.
And the woman snaps her body like a jigsaw
piece back into the hole she made
when she tore out of her home, just another
wound to mend, just another

episode of melancholia mentioned over
chamomile, forgotten by the time
the tea cups freeze to yawns inside
the cradle of the sink. The children
tip their heads against the pillows
and look as fragile as if their skulls
could crumble with the furious tap

of after-hour angst, when the trap
invites the rodent to a suicide, when
the needle's point trembles for its fix,
when the widow dresses hang themselves,
exhausted from the weight of stones.
If the children were awake they'd find
their mothers drifting in the air like errant

moths looking for a flower that blossoms
without light. They might even call them
beautiful if not for the oils that scurry down
their legs like piss. And if the women
were awake, they'd give each tiny lake
of blood beneath their feet a name.
But the broken world shows mercy

and each morning every person rises
none the wiser. The boys, fingering
their pockets stuffed with marbles, catch
the fleeting scent of something—pudenda
if they had the word, but they haven't
had it, so they run out to the road
to draw a circle on the dirt, a hole

dug in the center, an inverted nipple.
They play their game, pretending
that the aches inside their throats
are not their voices getting thicker.
If they begin to sound like grown-ups,
they begin to die. That's life
in the village without handsome

men: suddenly they wear the shoes
that lose their way. Some say
they journey North to waste
their days as kitchen slaves. Some say
they trade their organs for quick pay,
and that their shame means begging
on the city streets for gauze or cotton,

stitches or thread, to heal their surgeries
and stand upright again without
rattling like coins inside a cup.
And some believe they're seized
by soldier's fury and off they run to war
on foreign lands so dry the wind sucks out
the fluids in their faces. If they regret

their choice they cannot spit. And if they
yearn for what they left behind
they cannot cry. And if they scratch their cheeks
in sleep, dreaming that they're clawing
on the buttocks of their wives they cannot
bleed. Whatever path they take, whatever
headlines speak above the rumors, no one

knows for sure, though the silence
of their vanishing comes certainly. So too
succumbing to the deadness of the air.
In this village, and many others like it,
no one talks about the missing. Not a word
about the hat clinging to the only hook
in the wall, embedded question mark

not seen since—

Not a word about the pair of slippers
hibernating like two polar bears beneath
the sofa since—

Not a word about the extra chair
that sits fasting at the table losing
weight each season since—

If the picket fences stand like crosses
never mention it. If the yellow ribbons
cut the circulation off the trees
don't point it out. Find the fallen fruit
scattered like land mines on the ground
and eat it before it explodes, before
it betrays widow and orphan with its truth:

the men are never ever coming home.

CENTRAL AMERICAN ANXIETY GALLERY

Portrait One: Rebel Shot through the Eye

A bullet displaces his eyeball. He pierces
whatever he sees. My son, keep away
from broken glass, his mother used to plead.
And when she bows to bless him, the dead man shatters
her teeth. Now, she speaks through the asshole
of her lips, her tongue a mole that quivers at
the smallest hint of light. Unmoved, the son locks
his face to the sky as his mother fans the fire
in her jaw, yearning for a kiss from the next passerby.

Portrait Two: Decomposition Cycle

Bald chickens roam the dumping grounds.
They've pecked each other's combs off
and are angered by their ugly, pallid skulls.
What better comfort than pinching the pimples
off the hands that no longer feed them.
When the flesh slips off, the birds panic
at the sight of chicken bones. What betrayal
to be tricked into becoming cannibals again.
Worms boil in their stomachs clenched like fists.

Portrait Three: The Colonel Smoking on the Balcony

The tobacco is Cuban. The pipe fibula.
The dogs disguise themselves as mud
and will be spared the spit. Fireworks tonight—
Chinese ingenuity, American artistry.
The whole town comes out of hiding
now that the houses are gone. The show
begins: when the church explodes, children
scream; when the car explodes, children run;
when the children explode—

for Carolyn Forché

MORTUI VIVOS DOCENT

I

In the trunk, a blouse with breasts, a skirt
stretched open by hips that have shaken off
the last whiff of talcum powder at the pothole.
Clumsy dancer, dropping her shoe somewhere between
Mexicali and Calexico. If she were breathing
she'd let the whiskey tell the tale,
sultry syllable after sultry syllable—sí, mi amor.
Mummies are this century's mermaids,
rattling songs that will stop a heart. If we let them,
says the whale-eyed sailor, hands cuffed
to the steering wheel, mumbling the madness
of a man who found a woman whistling
beneath a Mexican moon—music so pretty
he just had to keep it from ruining the terrorist world.

II

This is how you ruin the terrorist world:
cut out the yellow heart of heaven,
drop the bloodless stars into the sea,
blind the women who sit to wonder on the shore.
I knew such a woman. I've kept her comb in my purse
after all these years, since the night my father found her
walking home from the Cachanilla hills.
You know the names, El Abanico, El Dollar, La Puta Eva
y El Pinche Adán, places so plump with pleasure
even the air turns to stupor, drunk with a sensory coma.
Clarification: she was not the body in the ruby corset,
not behind the pair of tassels, not inside the scent
of tangerines. My mother was the mop and the bucket
wiping off the fingerprints on the promiscuous wall.

III

This is how you press against the promiscuous wall:
drill the pair of diamonds on your back and moan;
hold your breath, float face-down on the vertical pool;
sway with the shadows set in motion by a swinging
chandelier—an angry father come to claim his child.
He did not catch me then, but he caught me
walking home, my knees still numb from dancing
with the men who love their mamacitas pink
and puckered as if they're sipping wine transparent
as the cloth across their thighs. What could I do
with lips like mine but kiss or whistle loud enough
to be the visible woman my overworked mother
never was? So, papi, keep your only son holy as you stuff
me in the trunk: I'm wearing mother's blouse, my mother's skirt.

Music Man

Oh father, oh music man
with a whistle instead of a coin
to toss on your walks,
keep these things for us
until we're ready to come home:

our baby teeth, fragments of bone
that rattle in a domino box.
Tuck it in your pocket but please
don't gamble it away
the way you lost our

christening gowns in poker.
We had outgrown them, true,
but what other proof
did we have that all seven
of our outfits could be stacked

and shuffled like a deck
of cards. Keep the bottle cap
opener hanging by a string.
Wear it like a locket
and stay collared to our after-school

bliss when we found you
underneath a tree that scattered
glass fruit around your feet.
The boys lined them up
for death by slingshot,

and the girls giggled
when the bodies shattered.
Take good care of our drawings,
our crooked handwriting
exercises, the scribbles of our names,

and sew a suit with sailboats
on the sleeves, a coat with Qs
sliding down a wire, and pants
that celebrate our prepubescent
autographs. And in your shoe—

don't tell us which! let us guess!—
save the coin you told us
came from China. It had a hole
in the middle because the merchants
slid their change on chopsticks.

We pictured them on market
Sundays holding up their earnings
like a shish kabob. We know
you hid the coin because all seven
of us wanted it and so you

took it with you. Or so I claimed.
Can I be blamed, oh father, oh story
man, for wanting to possess
the single thing that couldn't be shared?
You saw me slide it out

the window of your wallet
while you napped and didn't
snap to attention to complain.
Of all your sons and daughters
it is I who wanted to escape the most,

to anywhere. I learned the desperate
alchemy of flowering a barren day
with song from you, oh master.
A minstrel needs his freedom.
And so you let me take it.

FULL MOON ON THE NIGHT MY FATHER DIED

And then
silence.
No mouth

with the urge
for teeth.
A hand

without its switch.
Stones, not feet.
If a woman cries and is

not heard there was
no grief,
no leg collapsing at the knee,

no widow spilling open
like a sack of feed.
The moon,

having paused to see,
moves on:
just another night's

comma, just another eyelid
fluttering to the flash
of lightning the living

call father
or husband or son.
What the dead call

ante-sleep.

Unpeopled Eden

We died in your hills, we died in your deserts,
We died in your valleys and died on your plains.
We died 'neath your trees and we died in your bushes,
Both sides of the river, we died just the same.
"Plane Wreck at Los Gatos (Deportees)," Woody Guthrie

I

after the immigration raid

Beneath one apple tree the fruit
lies flung like the beads from
a rosary with a broken string.
Another tree stands amused
over the strangeness of a shoe
that pretends to be an apple
in its redness, though it'll never be
an apple with that lace stem
and a pit where a core should be.

The tree at the end of the row
will weep over the pillage
all week. Around its trunk, debris:
straw hats, handkerchief, a basket
going hungry for what's out

of reach. Somewhere in the orchard
a screech goes weaker by the hour.
A radio without paws, it cannot claw
its chords to end its suffering.

But silence comes, eventually,
and the apple trees will rest,
gathering the shadows to their roots
as the flame inside each apple
falls asleep. All the while, finches
perch among the branches—patient
vultures waiting for the fruit to rot.
For a wasp, intoxicated by the sugars,
this is the perfect place to nest.

The colony will thrive inside
decay: the apples softening until
their wrinkled skins begin to sink,
the seeds poking through like teeth.
The trees will sway without the wind
because the ground will boil
with larvae. A bird will feast
until it chokes and ants will march
into the belly through the beak.

II

after the ride by bus

A strand of hair pretends to be
a crack and sticks to glass. A piece
of thread sits on a seat, pretends
to be a tear. The bus makes believe
no one cried into their hands and smeared
that grief onto its walls. The walls
will keep the fingerprints a secret
until the sheen of oils glows by moon.
Rows of ghosts come forth to sing.

Until that keening rocks the bus
to rest, the fumes intoxicate
the solitary button—single witness
to the shuffling of feet and a final act
of fury: the yanking of a wetback's
shirt. The button popped right off
the flannel, marched in the procession
and then scurried to the side. The lesson:
if wounded, stay behind to die.

The bus breathes out the shapes
turned silhouettes turned scent
of salt and sweat. The steering wheel
unspools, every window shaking loose
the wetness of its glare. And now
a riddle squats over the parking lot:
What creature stands its ground
after evisceration? Roadkill. Clouds
close in to consume the afterbirth.

III

after the detention in the county jail

A mausoleum also keeps these gems:
precipitation that hardens into diamonds
on the cobweb stems, streams of urine
that shimmer like streaks of gold.
Lights coax out the coat of polish
on the floor and what's solid softens
into water stripped of ripples. Stilled
and empty, a river that has shoved
its pebbles down its throat.

The cell holds out three drops of blood
and will barter them for company,
hungry for the smell of men again. Janitor,
border guard or detainee, it's all the same
musk of armpit, garlic breath, oils
that bubble up from crack to tailbone,
scent of semen from the foreskin,
fungus from the toes. Without takers,
the keyhole constricts in the cold.

IV

after the deportation plane falls from the sky

A red-tailed hawk breaks through
the smoke and doesn't drop the way
the bodies did when the plane
began to dive and spat pieces of its
cargo out the door. No grace, the twitching
of such a great machine. No beauty to
its blackening inside the pristine
canvas of majestic blue—a streak of rage
made by a torch and not a paintbrush.

The hawk lands on the canyon
and snaps its neck in quick response
to the vulgar cracking on the boulders,
to the shrill of metal puncturing
the canyon, to the burst of flames
that traps a nest of mice within the lair
turned furnace, burning shriek, and hair.
Stunned host of sparrows scatters.
Fume of feathers, pollution in the air.

Poison in the lungs of all that breathes.
A darkness rises. The blue absorbs it
the way it dissipates a swarm after
the crisis of a shattered hive. Heaven
shows its mercy also, swallowing
the groan that spilled out of the hill.
No signs of tragedy by dusk
except a star splayed over rock,
the reek of fumes—a disemboweled god.

V

after the clean-up along Los Gatos Canyon

What strange flowers grow
in the shadow. Without petals
and with crooked twigs for stems.
The butterflies that pollinated them
were bits of carbon glowing
at the edge. The solitary lone wolf
spider doesn't dare to bite
the scorched caul on the canyon.
It packs its fangs for brighter lands.

The footprints drawn in black
do not match the footprints
in the orchard though they also
bear the weight of the unwanted.
The chain gang called upon to gather
the debris sang the Prison Blues
all afternoon: Inmate, deportee,
in your last attempt to flee
every bone splits into three.

VI

after the communal burial

Twenty-eight equals one
deportation bus equals one
cell in the detention center, one
plane-load of deportees, one
plunge into the canyon, one
body in the coffin although one
was a woman—sister not alone
anymore among the chaperone
of angels with wings of stone.

Manuel Merino, Julio Barrón,
Severo, Elías, Manuel Calderón,
Francisco, Santiago, Jaime, Martín,
Lupe, Guadalupe, Tomás, Juan Ruiz,
Alberto, Ramón, Apolonio, Ramón,
Luis, Román, Luis, Salvador,
Ignacio Navarro, Jesús, Bernabé,
Rosalío Portillo, María, y José.
Y un Deportado No Identificado.

No papers necessary to cross
the cemetery. The sun floods
the paths between tombs
and everything pushes out
into light. No shame to be
a cherub without a nose.
The wreath will not hide
its decay. Cement displays
its injuries with no regrets.

This is the place to forget
about labor and hardship and pain.
No house left to build, no kitchen
to clean, no chair on a porch, no
children to feed. No longing left
except a wish that will never come
true: Paint us back into the blank
sky's blue. Don't forget us
like we've forgotten all of you.

GILA

It's no curse
        dragging my belly across
                the steaming sand all day.
        I'm as thick as a callus
                that has shorn off its leg.

If you find me I can explain
        the trail made by a single limb.

        I am not a ghost.
Do not be afraid.

Though there are ghosts here—
        they strip down to wind
                or slump against rock to evaporate.

        Sometimes I crawl beneath the shedding,
backing up into the flesh pit for shade.
        Praise the final moisture of the mouth, its crown
                of teeth that sparkles with silver or gold.

I make a throne of the body
        until it begins to decay.

        And then I'll toss the frock—
death by hunger, death by heat—
        off the pimples of my skin.

Don't you dare come into my kingdom,
peasant, without paying respect on your knees!

What generous act did I commit
in my previous life, that I should be
                    rewarded with this paradise:

a garden in which every tree that takes root here
        drops its fruit eye-level to me.

Telegrama

(September 2006)

I write to you again:
      beloved brother, Apá has fallen ill.

But this time without a curandera dance,
without a magic pill to pry the lyrics off his tongue.

I have seen this dark silence before:

In the sickness that wraps around the cow
when it dries up and leaves the calf
looking blank as it suckles and suckles
because its mouth denies what its eyes know.

They say the owl will betray the outcome.
If it flaps its wings there will be breath.
If it stares and hoots at midnight—death.

Do you still laugh at our superstitions?
You, city boy as far away from us
as the cracks on the sky's glass we call stars,
you think we cannot hear you cry?

Your loneliness flaps louder than the echoing moth
trapped behind the shower curtain at night.
How it shreds the silence out of itself.

Our stepmother—father's last woman—
I hear the moth in her as well.

She keeps asking me,
        What were his last words?

I tell her,
        Stupid woman, he's not dead yet.
                He'll have a say all right when I tell him about this!

And then she wails into her hands.
Do you understand this strange jealousy of hers?

She wants me to tell her that our father
crooned her name and not our mother's
at the moment he slipped into his sleep.

She wants me to tell her that our father
loved her more than the dead love of his life.

I recognize now the cliff toward loss
in ways I have not before.

As I drove our father to the clinic
he said,
        Tell them I will miss them.

And then he slumped into the seat.

You know who he was thinking of.
Not of his first family. Not of his second either.
But of those figures from his childhood,
the ones he made us clap to in his silly songs.

Now that he sleeps the final traces
of that carnival have blown away. Gone
are the puppets wearing wooden shoes,
the fat clown the townspeople all thought
was the butcher disguised in paint

until the butcher showed up in a clean brown
suit, his hair bright with tonic and one
of the Huerta sisters at his side.

She must have made the same connection
by the way she let go of his arm
when they walked into the showman's tent
and the townspeople all turned to stare,
all of them undeceived at once.

Gone are the horses thin as girls,
and the girls who rode them, thin as candlesticks.

Gone is the strongman, his shoulders swollen
like golden bread. Adiós to the dwarf
who makes everyone feel large, and to the elephant
that crushes everyone down to size.

The droppings the animals left behind
have lost their smell and have hardened into rocks.

Gone is the lady who could hang by her ankle,
the man who could walk on a string,
both of them mothered by the same woman
spider, we were sure of it, by the weightlessness
of their bones. They must mate with each other
or risk coming apart beneath human passion.

And let's say our goodbyes to the lion,
remember that lion, beloved brother?
Apá said that it looked so bored
looking back at people, so unimpressed when
Chema shoved his fist into his own wide mouth.

The lion gazed indifferently, as if it had seen
Zacapu, this crumbling place, and its ordinary faces
many times before and so would never turn up
the lights inside its eyes again.

Could Apá have loved them more than us?
I suppose we know the answer to that.
Perhaps he will join them in that paradise
where musicians swim inside their compositions
until the world goes deaf,

until memory stops the tap-tap of fingertips
against the side of the head.

Beloved brother, Apá has fallen ill.

I am standing at the edge of his bed
and looking down. When I wipe away tears
I smudge myself into transparency—
my color coming off on my hard thumbs.

Are you vanishing as well, thinning out
like the orphan watching his father
looking back as he drives away?

BIRTHRIGHT

in the village
of your birth
cuts a wall
bleeds a border

in the heat
you cannot swim
in the rain
you cannot climb

in the north
you cannot be
cuts a paper
cuts a law

cuts a finger
finger bleeds
baby hungers
baby feeds

baby needs
you cannot go
you cannot buy
you cannot bring

baby grows
baby knows
bordercrossing
seasons bring

winter border
summer border
falls a border
border spring

for André

The Bordercrosser's Pillowbook

things that shine in the night

Fulgencio's silver crown—when he snores
the moon, coin of Judas, glaring
at the smaller metals we call stars
my buckle
the tips of my boots
the stones in my kidneys
an earring
a tear on the cheek
the forked paths of a zipper
the blade of the pocketknife triggering open
the blade of the pocketknife seducing the orange
the blade of the pocketknife salivating
the blade of the pocketknife
the word México
the word migra

things that are afraid to move when they sleep

the owls carved on rock
Fulgencio
me

things that forget their shapes

snakes
our bedding
our clothes
the shadows twitching by the fire
the skin of the rabbit—its flesh
an apple
the orange
the jacaranda behind the house
the roof—the clothesline—the curtains
the door that swells in the heat
the pipes that shrink in the cold
the couch—the table—the lamp
the dominoes
the dishes
the children—the wife—the neighbors
memory

things that make noises at dawn

the sun as it rips away from the horizon
the sun as it pounds against my skin
the sand moaning with my weight
my weight moaning with the sand
the stones in my kidneys
children waking up in the homes we left behind
the footfalls—the footprints—the foot
Fulgencio's prayer without saints—or God

things that open like flowers in daylight

Fulgencio's eyes
Fulgencio's mouth—as he yawns
the buttons on his shirt
the orange peel—the campsite—the desert—the world
the jacaranda behind the house
the roof—the clothesline—the curtains
the door that swells in the heat
the pipes that shrink in the cold
the couch—the table—the lamp
the dominoes
the dishes
the children—the wife—the neighbors
memory
the white sparks in my brain
the red sparks in my heart
the stones in my kidneys

things that travel at the speed of silence

air
sand
heat
light
grief
memory
thought
Fulgencio
me

things I would say to Fulgencio if I could say them

erase our shadows
carve our names in stone
let us watch for comets while we rest
let us not make wishes that will not come true
your shoes abandoned you the way I never will
let me fan the fires on your toes
these are the final drops of my fear—drink them
these are the final drops of my fever—drink them
these are the final drops of my love—drink them
hold me—I have a flame on my tongue
hold me—you are a mouth of water
hold me—we taste of tangerines
hold me

things I want to polish clean

an apple—and another one—and another
my buckle
the tips on my boots
Fulgencio's forehead
our tracks on the sand
the ring on my finger
the horizon—its infestation of green cars
the word wetback
the voice—the bullhorn—the officer
Fulgencio's tears of shame—the sores on his toes
the sound of static—of running motors—of running men
the jacaranda behind the house
the roof—the clothesline—the curtains
the door that swells in the heat
the pipes that shrink in the cold
the couch—the table—the lamp
the dominoes
the dishes
the children—the wife—the neighbors
memory
the stones in my kidneys
the stones in my kidneys
I'd set them in gold—
I'd set them in gold—try to wear them like teeth

La Pelona as Birdwoman

Tonight
I dared to crawl
beneath the sheets

to be nailed down
around me,
waiting for my lover, she

who enters
without knocking, she
who will unstitch

my every seam
along my thigh,
my side, my armpit.

She who carves
a heart out of the heart
and drops it

down her throat.
Sweet surrender this
slow death in sleep

as I dream
the lovemaking
is autopsy. How else

will I be hers
completely? Be her
treasure box I said:

a trove of pearls
and stones, the ding
of coins cascading

through her fingers.
The bird over her shoulder
not a parrot, but an owl

to be my mirror
when I close my eyes
and shape a moon-white

bowl out of my face
where she can wash
the hooks of her caress.

Still with water, I'm
one more thing to penetrate.
I'm one more spill

of secrets on the floor.
A puddle glowing green—
she doesn't have to be a sleuth

to see I've taken
all the antifreeze.
A puddle thick with red—

she'll kneel
next to my wounds
and pray for me,

a string of pigeon skulls
her rosary.
By dawn our bone pièta

breaks out of its shadow,
unleashes its cicada cry.
My daughters drag

their bodies, bruised as bats,
out to the light
and burst into flames

like marigolds.
The crows will leap
down from the trees

to pick them clean.
And my beloved bride,
beloved wife, will laugh

until it hurts her teeth.
It's the feather
of her tongue—

eleventh finger—
I recall
and not the catheter

while the priest recites
his holy dribble
and the churchyard

worker takes a leak.
My sons hold up
their chins with pride

that they have done
their part to hide
my suicide:

they've clipped
my fingertips
to lose the track

back to my prints.
But my beloved knows:
she crouches

on the highest branch
and drops an egg
that cracks my coffin.

Concussion light
squirms through
and I'm in heaven once again—

those times
we screwed like hen
and rooster: I

the squawking chicken
blacking out, and she
the hammering cock.

In the Village of Missing Sons

The old do not call themselves old,
they call themselves dead. They call
themselves forgotten and silent, the footprints
made by water that evaporate and erase,
leaving the ground thirsty for contact
all over again. They call themselves
banished, abandoned, invisible—

the winter that welcomes no guests
though it pleads for them, clearing
wide paths on streets that grow white as
bone grieving its decomposed flesh.
A wooden bench rots in the park
without a story to tell. A leg bends at the knee
without a church. And off in the distance

a body melts into the light like the final
whisper from the dying man's mouth: Oh sheets,
give me more glorious buttercups that bleed.
Oh crow, morning's ubiquitous beggar,
ask me for a piece of bread, please,
please, please. Oh wall with a clock
for a mole, I'll never again turn away

from the sight of your three bristly hairs.
But no one hears such supplications
or notices the weakest of the weak wearing
moths instead of buttons, knots of yarn
instead of throats, and screwing bottle caps
into their sockets to keep the milky eyes
from leaking out. There's already a woman

haunting the streets with white feathers
on her head, and when she cries the tears
harden on her cheeks like chicken shit.
She gave birth to a son who broke like an egg
beneath a military heel, and what a surprise
to find out, after all these years, she was a hen.
She perches on a shoe at night and pretends

it's an umbilical cord and not a lace.
What a disgrace to flaunt her childlessness
that way, complain the mothers who must scratch
around the pictures of their decorated dead—
Oh rosary of baby teeth, Oh bellybutton crucifix—
in private. The fathers cluster at the bar to coat
their battle scars with gin. One cradles a bottle

of wine and tickles its label with his finger,
while another tries to coax the cork into its neck.
In the corner three shadows rock side to side,
murmuring a lullaby, and the bartender nods off
into dream because, at fifty-five, he's the youngest
in the village and sits closer to the memory
of infancy than anyone. He'll climb atop your lap

if it will make you chuckle, he'll let you
share your kisses with a slice of pie, he'll
even—but only for the price of a potato—let you
watch him suck his thumb. No one judges him
when he slips into his truck pajamas and begins to nest.
In the village of missing sons there are sadder
scenes than that: the mayor scolding the mice

for eating sugar and refusing to brush
their teeth; the schoolteacher reading a fable
to a row of coffee cups to usher them to sleep;
the doctor's wife pinching her nipple numb
over the orchid when it's time to feed.
In every yard tricycles rise like gravestones,
and in the fall the festival of raking leaves—

an annual archeological dig for a marble,
a miniature wheel, or the plastic head of a doll—
any toy at all that will prove that boys
once inhabited the land. One day a couple found
a slingshot, and for a week they were crowned
with the most coveted of artifacts: birthday
party hats, sun-bleached and slightly bent on top,

still celebrated symbols of the times of laughter.
But before the couple gave them back, he shot her
from behind, then shot himself, their blood
sprinkled on the frosting of uneaten cake.
No one wore the party hats again and the people
cursed the suicides for taking that away.
And curse the war with its appetite

for adolescent hearts that still contract
at the sight of partial nudity. Curse the men
who wrap their flags around their eyes to bind
themselves to loyalty. Curse the women
who allow their sons to murder other women's
sons and call it victory. And on this village
of the stupid and the blind this curse:

May you never know the magic of a child
who can point and pierce a cloud, who can
squint and cage the parakeet before it flees the house,
who can bite into a cherry and roll the world
inside his mouth, who can color in the autumn's brown,
who can pinch the sun between two fingers
and then, with childish mercy, let it out.

May the miniatures inside your memories—
little socks, little shoes, little belts and little
gloves—pop like seeds and disperse into the wind.
May the shrills of giggling, the shrieks of tantrums
sink into the smiles of hoof prints filling up
with mud. May the bite marks on your arms,
around the edges of the pastries, lose their baby teeth

and rot as you yourselves decay each childless day
in the village of missing sons. May you
call yourselves extinct and collapse among
the cribs turned rib cages, among the sticky tar pits
that used to be the swimming pools. May your shadows
vanish from the center outward and then roam
their final hours as the outlines of neglect

in the village without a playground or a school,
in the village where you drape your sagging skins
across the windows for a last encounter
with the fading light, in the village where bodies
and buildings marry into rubble and can't even
birth the dust, in the village without headstones,
without history, without names and without ghosts.

CASA

I am not your mother, I will not be moved
by the grief or gratitude of men
who weep like orphans at my door.
I am not a church. I do not answer
prayers but I never turn them down.

Come in and kneel or sit or stand,
the burden of your weight won't lessen
no matter the length of your admission.
Tell me anything you want, I have to listen
but don't expect me to respond

when you tell me you have lost your job
or that your wife has found another love
or that your children took their laughter
to another town. You feel alone and empty?
Color me surprised! I didn't notice they were gone.

Despite the row of faces pinned like medals
to my walls, I didn't earn them.
The scratches on the wood are not my scars.
If there's a smell of spices in the air
blame the trickery of kitchens

or your sad addiction to the yesterdays
that never keep no matter how much you believe
they will. I am not a time capsule.
I do not value pithy things like locks
of hair and milk teeth and ticket stubs

and promise rings—mere particles
of dust I'd blow out to the street if I could
sneeze. Take your high school jersey
and your woman's wedding dress away
from me. Sentimental hoarding bothers me.

So off with you, old couch that cries
in coins as it gets dragged out to the porch.
Farewell, cold bed that breaks its bones
in protest to eviction or foreclosure or
whatever launched this grim parade

of exits. I am not a pet. I do not feel
abandonment. Sometimes I don't even see you
come or go or stay behind. My windows
are your eyes not mine. If you should die
inside me I'll leave it up to you to tell

the neighbors. Shut the heaters off
I do not fear the cold. I'm not the one
who shrinks into the corner of the floor
because whatever made you think
this was a home with warmth isn't here

to sweet-talk anymore. Don't look at me
that way, I'm not to blame. I granted
nothing to the immigrant or exile
that I didn't give a bordercrosser or a native
born. I am not a prize or a wish come true.

I am not a fairytale castle. Though I
used to be, in some distant land inhabited
by dreamers now extinct. Who knows
what happened there? In any case, good
riddance, grotesque fantasy and mirth.

So long, wall-to-wall disguise in vulgar
suede and chintz. Take care, you fool,
and don't forget that I am just a house,
a structure without soul for those whose
patron saints are longing and despair.

Señorita Juárez

1.

       Doña Lencha's mint leaves crushed
to the bottom of the teacup
       did not predict this heat.
The crucifix melts to a tear on my cheek.

2.

       Body in the desert looks as if she's
waving goodbye. The slipper fled
       from her ballerina fantasy.
Farewell symmetry that snaps at the leg.

3.

       In the end we are like the shark
that swims with a treasure chest
       in its belly. Poachers slice us open,
extract a string of kidney stones, a license plate.

4.

       A strong wind scatters the linen
off the line. And then the burdensome task
       of collecting clothespins like teeth
while the skeletal wires snicker from above.

5.

       Discards from the rummage sale:
wagon without wheels, a coil of soiled rope,
       a doll grinning at her nudity—her call
for help, lettered blocks tumbling out of reach.

6.

       The cleaning lady said that
television was a prison for beauty
       queens. So she cracked ours open,
set the poor shivering women free.

7.

Static, if it had shape. Darkness,
if it had song. The old radio in the kitchen
with a red doily like a bloody bib.
All afternoon the newsman's dribble.

8.

Dropped in the living room, a tin
of buttons weeps all morning long—
the buttonholes suddenly aware
that they've been eviscerated from the thread.

9.

A fruit falls from the branch.
It will not scream. Sound tightens like
a fetus at the pit. Pity the Christian
burial among the scorn of tumbleweed and light.

for Alicia Gaspar de Alba

NOTES

"The Soldier of Mictlán": Mictlán is the region of the dead in
Mexica / Aztec mythology.

"Mortui Vivos Docent": The phrase is Latin for "Let the dead teach
the living," motto of the morgue.

"Unpeopled Eden": Chris Mahin, commenting on the occasion of the
60th anniversary of "Plane Wreck at Los Gatos (Deportees)" by
Woody Guthrie, wrote the following account:

The fire began over Los Gatos Canyon. It started in the left engine-driven
fuel pump. The plane crashed 20 miles west of Coalinga, California, on
January 29, 1948.

There were 32 people on board that day, but the names of only four are
recorded for history. The newspaper articles about the crash describe an
accident involving a Douglas DC-3 carrying immigrant workers from
Oakland, California to the El Centro, California Deportation Center.
Those accounts give the name of the plane's pilot (Frank Atkinson),
and co-pilot (Marion Ewing). They mention the name of the stewardess
(Bobbie Atkinson) and the guard (Frank E. Chapin). However, the
newspaper stories do not include the names of any of the 27 men or of
the one woman who were passengers on that flight, victims who were
buried in a mass grave at Holy Cross Cemetery in Fresno, California. The
newspaper reports simply dismiss them as "deportees."

The twenty-eight deportees to whom this poem is dedicated (que en paz descansen):

Julio Barrón, Manuel Calderón, Francisco Durán, Santiago Elisandro, Rosalío Estrada, Bernabé García, Jaime A. Guardajo, Severo Lara, Elías Macías, José Macías, Tomás Márquez, Luis Medina, Manuel Merino, Luis Mirando, Ignacio Navarro, Martín Navarro, Román Ochoa, Ramón Pérez, Apolonio Placencia, Ramón Portillo, Guadalupe Ramírez, Alberto Raygoza, Guadalupe Rodríguez, María Rodríguez, Juan Ruiz, Salvador Sandoval, and Jesús Santos. And to the Unidentified One.

"La Pelona as Birdwoman": "La Pelona" is the Mexican nickname for death. Literally it means "the bald woman."

Acknowledgments

These poems first appeared in: *American Poetry Review, BorderSenses, Cura, Diode Poetry Journal* (online), *La Fovea* (online), *NewBorder, The Packinghouse Review, Palabra, Poetry Kanto* (Yokohama, Japan), *The Rome Review,* and *The Southern Review.*

"The Soldier of Mictlán" was produced as a broadside by Roni Gross on the occasion of a poetry reading on December 7, 2007, at the Center for Book Arts in New York City.

"Mortui Vivos Docent" appears in *Stranger at Home: American Poetry with an Accent,* edited by Andrey Gritsman et al, New York, NY: Interpoezia, Inc. & Numina Press, 2008.

"In the Village of Missing Fathers" appears in *Fire and Ink: An Anthology of Social Action Writing,* edited by Frances Paine Adler, Debra Busman and Diana García, Tucson, AZ: University of Arizona Press, 2009.

"Central American Anxiety Gallery," "Gila," "Mortui Vivos Docent," and "La Pelona as Birdwoman" appear in *Me No Habla Con Acento: Contemporary Latino Poetry,* edited by Emanuel Xavier, Hulls Cove, ME: Rebel Sartori Press, 2011.

"Gila" also appears in *A Face to Meet the Faces: An Anthology of Contemporary Persona Poetry,* edited by Stacy Lynn Brown and Oliver de la Paz, Akron, OH: University of Akron Press, OH, 2012.

Many thanks to María Meléndez for her editorial comments, to Eduardo C. Corral for help with the order, and much gratitude to my brother Alex, my sisters Maythee and Lizzy, and Mami. To my dear friends, deep affection.

Rigoberto González is the author of thirteen books of poetry and prose, and the editor of *Camino del Sol: Fifteen Years of Latina and Latino Writing*. He is the recipient of Guggenheim and NEA fellowships, winner of the American Book Award, The Poetry Center Book Award, The Shelley Memorial Award of The Poetry Society of America, a grant from the New York Foundation for the Arts, and the Barnes & Noble Writers for Writers Award. He is contributing editor for *Poets & Writers Magazine*, on the executive board of directors of the National Book Critics Circle, and is associate professor of English at Rutgers-Newark, the State University of New Jersey.